In Our LIVERPOOL HOME

Outside fishmarket in Great Charlotte Street, c. 1890 (C. R. Inston).

Right: nature outing from Aspen Grove school, 1914 (J. G. Legge).

In Our
LIVERPOOL HOME

Brian Walker
and
Ann Hinchliffe

Blackstaff Press

Published by Blackstaff Press Limited, 255A Upper Newtownards Road, Belfast BT4 3JF.

Designed by Wendy Dunbar

ISBN 0 85640 173 0

Printed in Ireland by Cahill 1976 Limited.

George's Dock, 1891, with St Nicholas' church and the Tower Buildings in the background (Arthur Priestley). This, of course, is the site of the present day Liver Buildings.

Contents

Photographers' tents on the sands at New Brighton, c. 1890 (Francis Frith).

Introduction

It is difficult for us today to imagine what life was really like in Liverpool at the turn of this century. Contemporary writers have left us valuable records in the form of reports, newspapers and novels. But for the most vivid and evocative depiction of the experience of life at this time, we must surely turn to the work of the photographers of the period. Through their photographs it is possible to see again the people of this past age, in the streets, at work, at leisure and among their friends. Thanks to the efforts of these remarkable artists, we are able to recapture brief moments of this earlier Liverpool, a city with many of the same streets and physical features as today, but with a very different way of life from our own.

In this book the photographs of a number o Liverpool photographers have been brough together to give a picture of the many differen faces of this thriving city at the turn of th century. The presentation of the material is ver different from other books of old Liverpoo photographs inasmuch as the pictures ar arranged by photographer. Much time has bee spent identifying the persons behind the photo graphs and in most cases, although not all, w have been able to give information on the indiv duals responsible for these photographs. Five c the chapters are devoted to the work of particular photographer; chapters two and fou contain the work of two photographers, whi chapter eight consists of the work of five different photographers. We believe that this method of presentation enhances the value of the photographs, emphasising the talent of the artists responsible and illustrating their special interests.

Each photographer covers a different subject or theme. Some of the photographs used in this book have been used elsewhere but we believe they are worth seeing again in this new context. Most of the photographs, however, have not been published before. All were taken between 1880 and 1914. As well as the detailed captions which have been provided for the photographs, suitable advertisements, extracts from newspapers, novels and reports have been included to give a useful contemporary perspective to the photographs.

By the time of our period photography was well established in Liverpool. Only a few weeks after the founding of the Royal Photographic Society in London, the Liverpool Photographic Society was formed at a meeting in Lime Street on 9 March 1853. Subsequently the Liverpool Society was merged with the Historic Society of Lancashire and Cheshire but in 1863 the Liverpool Amateur Photographic Society was formed. By 1898 the society had a membership of 350. Professional photography also developed in the city. In 1915 there were sixty-six photographic firms in Liverpool, employing 350 people in a variety of capacities.

The work of the photographers selected for this book gives a broad and varied picture of Liverpool life. From the camera of the famous professional photographer, Francis Frith, we receive his fine photographs of the main thoroughfares of Liverpool, while through the work of another professional photographer, Arthur Priestley, we catch a special glimpse of the port and its shipping which was the basis of the city's prosperity. But in addition to the grand public views of Frith and Priestley, we have photographs by others like Thomas Burke and C. F. Inston dealing with street life, children, markets and trams.

The idea for the title of the book was inspired by the Spinners' song 'In my Liverpool home', and we hope it captures the spirit of the book. This is the familiar Liverpool of over sixty years ago. It is a city which then as today was impressive and solid, as well as friendly, colourful and intimate. It is a city in which the inhabitants had intense pride. The selection of the photographs is our personal one, but we hope the book will convey to others something of the vitality and charm of 'our Liverpool home' in this earlier age which we have found so powerfully conveyed in these photographs.

Brian Walker
Ann Hinchliffe

7

The Walker Art Gallery, c. 1895. On the left is the Steble Fountain.

Cityscape

The work of Francis Frith was probably more widely known in late Victorian Britain than that of any other photographer. His commercial photographic business had over one million prints by the 1890s and included photographs covering most cities and towns in the country as well as parts of Europe and the Middle East. The photographs in this chapter are typical of his city work, showing broad street scenes, important buildings and well known views. All appear to have been taken in the 1880s and 1890s and so provide us with a fascinating view of the city of Liverpool at the height of its Victorian splendour. Some of these photographs, of course, may have been taken by Frith's assistants but all show clearly the Francis Frith approach and interest.

By the 1880s Frith was based at Reigate, Surrey, but earlier in his life he had important connections with Liverpool. Born at Chesterfield in Derbyshire in 1822, he moved *circa* 1845 to Liverpool where he began a wholesale grocery business and then a printing company. He appears to have started taking photographs in 1850 and in 1853 he was founder member of the Liverpool Photographic Society. Commercial success allowed him to turn full time to photography in 1856. Three years later he established a commercial photographic studio at Reigate. This business expanded rapidly, supplying photographs for postcards, books and guides, and providing various other photographic services. Frith died in 1898.

The Liverpool which Frith photographed in the 1880s and 1890s was the second biggest city in Britain and the largest seaport. With justice it was known as the second city of the empire. The basis of Liverpool's prosperity was her port and trade. During the nineteenth century vast new dock and harbour facilities were developed and the port received large imports of goods such as cotton, tobacco, wool and grain, and exported many types of manufactured products. Good communications by canal, road and railway linked the city with the rest of Great Britain. Liverpool was also the main passenger port of the United Kingdom. In the course of the nineteenth century a number of industries arising out of the commerce of the port were established, such as flourmilling, sugar-refining and, at nearby Birkenhead, shipbuilding.

With all this commercial prosperity Liverpool expanded rapidly. Municipal boundaries were extended a number of times between the 1830s and the early twentieth century. The population grew from 165,000 in 1831 to 380,000 in 1855, and to over 724,000 in 1905. Liverpool was granted city status in 1880. During the second half of the nineteenth century much redevelopment occurred in the city centre. New shops, business premises and offices were built. Neighbouring areas such as Birkenhead and Wallasey also expanded; as well as housing workers from Liverpool they developed their own commerce and industries. Municipal services were improved and extended. Communications within Liverpool and with neighbouring towns were continually improved.

In this Victorian metropolis important new institutions and public buildings were constructed. During the 1860s and 1870s the museum, the Walker Art Gallery, the William Brown Library and the Picton Reading Room were opened. A university college was inaugurated in 1881 and in 1903 it became a university in its own right. A number of extensive public parks were laid out. Many charitable bodies existed and during the Victorian era new hospitals, infirmaries, libraries and schools were established, often due to the enterprise of individuals. Plans were drawn up by both the Anglican and Catholic churches for the construction of cathedrals but building operations did not get under way on either until the twentieth century. There was a thriving cultural life in the city, with many musical societies, orchestras and theatres.

Following page: Liverpool guide books of the late nineteenth century began almost invariably with an account of Lime Street, seen here c. 1890. On the left is St George's Hall, the most prestigious Victorian public building in the city. Designed by the architect, Harvey Lonsdale Elmes, when only in his twenties, the hall contained law courts and a magnificent concert hall which became the setting for meetings, concerts and recitals. It was opened in 1854. In the distance, to the left of the Wellington memorial, are two later Victorian buildings — the Walker Art Gallery, opened in 1877, and the county sessions court, opened in 1884. In sharp contrast to these buildings in the classical mode, the North-Western Hotel, seen on the right, was built in French renaissance style and opened in 1871 as part of Lime Street station. Beside the North-Western Hotel are the well known Oyster Rooms and the Royal Hotel, two of the many smaller hotels and places of entertainment to be found in the Lime Street area. In the centre of the street are various horsedrawn trams, hansom cabs and carts.

Right: Church Street, 1889. Above: Lord Street, 1889. These two streets formed the main thoroughfare in the city centre. They contained many large stores and business premises. In Church Street can be seen the Compton Hotel, built in the 1860s as a drapery store and converted into a hotel in 1872-3. Some of the buildings in these pictures still survive today, but usually with modern shop fronts; for example, Compton's is now Marks and Spencer.

BUSY CHURCH STREET

There is no street in Liverpool so analagous to a London thoroughfare as Church Street, and there is no season of the year when Church Street is so busy as that of Christmas. People make a habit of walking down Church Street. There are the usual feminine denizens, who make a practice of taking a daily inventory of the window attractions of the various millinery establishments, who can tell you in chronological order every advance made in millinery by Madame de Plosshe et Cie, or the latest developments in Zouaves, and Raglans, exhibited at the Liverpool, Bootle, and Paris Mantle Emporia. Then there is the usual sprinkling of business men, who, with difficulty and patience, pick their adjectively garnished way through a phalanx of feminine impedimenta and write to the press all kinds of impossible suggestions for the aerial transmission of pedestrian traffic, instead of crossing over to the other and almost unused side. Some people are never satisfied. Do the parading girls attract them there?

Liverpool Review 28 December 1901.

Bold Street, c. 1890. This street, overlooked by the high tower of St Luke's church, boasted some of the best shops in Liverpool, with fin window displays of drapery, millinery and jewellery. Local pride in the street was expressed in a popular poem of the 1890s which ended with the lines:

> *In London, they*   *It matters not,*
> *Have got the Strand,*   *For Dicky Sams*
> *The finest place*   *Have also got*
> *In all the land,*   *An equally*
> *For fashions*   *Delightful spot*
> *Camaraderie;*   *In Bold Street*
> *But still, for us*   *Promenaderie.*

'Dicky Sam' was the local nickname for an inhabitant of Liverpool.

The Central Railway Station, c. 1890. This station at the bottom of Ranelagh Street was the terminus of the Cheshire Lines. At the lower central station a connection could be made with the Mersey electric railway. The railways were a vital component of the city's transport, there being no less than 108 stations in the Liverpool district in 1899. On the right of the photograph can be seen part of the Lyceum club, a fine early nineteenth century building, which contained a private club, newsroom and library with nearly 60,000 books in 1883.

South east view of the Exchange flags and buildings, c. 1890. Built in 1867, these exchange buildings formed three parts of a square; the town hall formed the fourth part. Within the newsrooms of the exchange, merchants and brokers connected with the trade interests of the city met to conduct business. Formerly, merchants had auctioned their goods in the square in front of the exchange, known as the flags. By the 1880s however, cotton brokers were the only people who still carried out their business in the open; in 1896 this practice ceased when they moved to Brown's Buildings and then to their own cotton exchange, opened in 1906. The famous Wyatt monument to Nelson can be seen in the foreground of the photograph. The men gathering on the left of the square are probably attending a cotton auction. This activity on the flags was described colourfully in an 1886 guide to the city:

'The staple trade of Liverpool is still largely carried on, for reasons best known to those engaged in it, in the open air, and the well dressed and earnest looking men who crowd together in one corner of the Flags — objects of curiosity, doubtless, to the uninitiated stranger — are deep in "spots", "futures" and other mysteries of the cotton market. All seems quiet enough as we look on, but momentous issues often depend on what goes on in that corner — a rise or fall there may not only make or mar the fortunes of those immediately engaged, but indirectly affect the well being of thousands, who never saw a handful of the raw material in their lives; and every pulsation of that market repeats itself all around the globe.'

The visitors' illustrated guide to Liverpool on the occasion of the 1886 international trade exhibition (Liverpool, 1886), p 16.

Customs House, Canning Place, c. 1885. The Exchange Buildings and the Customs House were together the commercial heart of Liverpool. In the Customs House were based the customs, the headquarters of the post office and the Mersey Docks and Harbour Board offices. By the early twentieth century, however, the two last named bodies had moved to new premises. The Customs House, opened in the 1830s, was destroyed by bombing in 1941.

36662 FF&C?

18

The great activity to be seen on the landing stage was described amusingly in an article in the Liverpool Review of 22 June 1889:

EIGHT HOURS ON THE LANDING STAGE

'Life on the Landing Stage'' written up on the *Review* some time ago created unwonted interest far and wide.

''A few hours on the Landing Stage'' runs in another groove; it also has its attractions. Let me try to elaborate a few of them.

During the summer moths the Landing Stage is seen at its best from mid-day until 7 or 8 o'clock at night. Through the intervening hours the bridges and approaches are thronged with continuous streams of people on pleasure bent. The greater number of this day-by-day procession are trippers from inland towns, to whom a look at the Mersey and the ships is next to a peep into heaven, and our own Liverpudlian mammas who, when father, dear old struggle, is toiling over his desk, or dodging six months' bills, take upon themselves the pleasurable duty of giving the children an airing.

Arrived on the Landing Stage, the half-dozen streams of health-hunting holiday seekers converge towards the ferry-boats, those plying to Egremont and New Brighton getting the great bulk of the passengers.

Going down the gangway on to the boats there is, as a matter of course, a good deal of clinging to mamma's jacket or dress, and a chorus of maternal voices, while a score of maternal eyes anxiously look round, call out, ''Now, Charlie, mind where you are going!'' ''Are you behind me, Cissie?'' and a dozen other directions besides.

The number of city men, clerks, and apprentices who stroll the length of the stage during the dinner hours, say from 12.30 to 2.30, is very considerable. They come down for a ''blow'' and, contrary to all rules of etiquette and menu cards, to take ''air soup'' after their chops, hot-pot, and rhubarb pudding. Many others of all sorts and conditions of men, from the seedy, greasy loafer and unemployed to the city merchant, take a delight in seeing the coasting boats arrive and depart and the tenders leave for the ocean greyhounds lying in mid river.

To see a saloon tender leave the Prince's is a valuable as well as an interesting experience. In one week, on the few yards of stage in proximity to the Customs shed, you can rub shoulders with more real live lords and ladies, and more aristocratic, dramatic, and fashionable notabilities than you can anywhere in England, the Metropolis excepted, in twelve months. The air of luxury and wealth which surrounds a saloon tender when she is casting off for a ''society greyhound'' is a sharp reminder of the gulf which divides the toiler from the capitalist, the poor from the affluent.

Of the boatmen and hangers-on who dawdle about the Landing Stage from early morn to dewy eve, I can tell nothing that is not well known; the boatmen dawdle about for jobs, the hangers-on dawdle, dawdle, dawdle, for anything gratis from a copper to a quid of tobacco. The hangers-on who really contrive to enjoy themselves are the hatless, bare-footed, ragged urchins, whose sole ambition in life appears to be to live with dirty, crusty hands and face and dodge round policemen. They are remarkably expert at the latter amusement, and on the Landing Stage live in an Elysium of laughter, horse-play and dodgery. P.C. No.— and a few others of the blue-coated fraternity know this to their cost. I must admit that I like these young ragamuffins ''baiting,'' and so do the bystanders.

Two children playing in the street, c. 1895 (Burke).

Street children

The rich and vibrant Liverpool which welcomed visitors to its broad streets, elegant premises and bustling docks had been created and fashioned by a world of adults to serve the older generation. There existed, however, living and playing at its feet, another world which many would have noticed but which few recorded. Children were everywhere in Liverpool, playing and selling wares around the streets, begging by the landing stage and tugging on mothers' aprons. But while the grand public side of this expanding Liverpool was recorded by many photographers, only a few concerned themselves with the lives of these children. Thomas Burke and C. F. Inston were two such photographers who took particular delight in portraying the street children.

Who exactly Thomas Burke was is not certain. Given the type of photograph which he took, it is likely that he is the Thomas Burke (1865-1941) who was a city councillor for Vauxhall from 1898 until the 1920s. He took a keen interest in the problems of street trading, children's employment, housing and other leading social problems of the day. He worked as a poultry and fish salesman in St John's market. Our other photographer, Charles Frederick Inston, lived at Belmont Avenue, Newsham Park, and ran a printing and stationery business. He was a fellow of the Royal Photographic Society and president of the Liverpool Amateur Photographic Society. He died in 1917.

The children whom Burke and Inston photographed in the streets came usually from impoverished backgrounds. In the middle of the nineteenth century, the rate of infant mortality in Liverpool's poor quarters had been very high and though steps were taken to alleviate the situation, conditions were still deplorable fifty years later. The infant mortality rate for England over the period 1881-90 was 142 per 100 births while for Liverpool it was 183; in the Vauxhall ward, it was 264 in 1891. Medical opinion attributed this high mortality rate to overcrowded and badly ventilated housing, errors in feeding, inadequate clothing and violence due to parents' drunkenness. Parents and children often slept in the same bed and deaths were sometimes caused by suffocation as the result of a mother or father rolling over on a child.

Even when a child survived the earliest years, he had to face a very deprived childhood, with poor food, clothing and housing. Compared to other cities, Liverpool, through its council, private individuals and charities, did make a reasonable effort to improve conditions for these children. Father Nugent and Canon Major Lester were two leading social reformers in Liverpool in the second half of the nineteenth century who concerned themselves with the plight of children, providing them with homes, clothes and food. The first branch in Britain of the Society for the Prevention of Cruelty to Children was formed in Liverpool in 1883. Others sought to improve the condition of children by urging improvements in housing and employment, or by advocating temperance. Eleanor Rathbone was a prominent reformer of the early twentieth century, urging the abolition of casual labour and the provision of family allowances as a means to alleviate, among other things, domestic conditions for children; her ideas on family allowances were of national importance.

By the turn of the century, children up to the age of eleven had to attend school from 9 — 12 a.m. and from 1.30 — 4 p.m., while between eleven and thirteen years of age children were obliged to attend for only half the day and could be employed for the other half; this last named practice known as 'half-timing' was abolished only in 1918. Truancy was a problem although the general attendance rate rose from 72.1 per cent in 1870 to 87.1 in 1900; in the poorer quarters the attendance rate was much lower.

Many of these truant children and others in their early teens were involved in street trading for their personal survival or to make much needed extra money for their families. In an attempt to protect children involved in street trading, the corporation brought in special legislation in 1898 requiring these children to be clothed properly and to be licensed for this work. The 1903 children's employment act was a further step in protecting children at work.

The best known account of the harsh lives of nineteenth century Liverpool street children is of course Silas Hocking's *Her Benny*. First published in 1879 and subsequently re-issued in many editions, this novel tells in a sentimental yet compelling way the adventures of two destitute children in Victorian Liverpool. It is appropriate to end this introduction with an extract from *Her Benny* which tells of Benny's efforts to survive.

'Benny's first thought now was to secure a substantial breakfast, which was by no means a difficult matter. That done, he made his way towards the docks, in the hope that he might get employment of some kind. But to a little friendless lad, without character or recommendation, employment was not so easily obtained. Most of those whom he addressed did not condescend to notice his question in any way. A few asked him what he could do, and when he replied, "Anything," the invariable answer was, "That means nothing," and he was sent about his business. In fact, there seemed to be no work in the whole line of docks that a child of his age was capable of doing. And night found him worn out with fatigue, and with a sadly lightened pocket.

'However, he kept up his heart as well as he could, and sought rest and sleep in a damp cellar upon some dirty straw, which for the payment of twopence he shared with a dozen other lads, who appeared to be as friendless as himself. That night he slept the sleep of the innocent and weary, and awoke next morning strengthened and refreshed, to find that all his companions had left and that his pockets were empty.'

Her Benny (London, 1879; new impression, Liverpool, 1968).

Group on doorstep near Gerard Street, 1895 (Burke). This is probably a family group consisting of the grandmother surrounded by her daughter and grandchildren. Families living in the poorer areas, especially around Scotland and Vauxhall Roads, were usually large in spite of the high juvenile death rate. Family ties were strong, particularly those between mother and daughter, and married daughters often lived close to their former homes. Children were very much taken for granted in this type of environment: the girls stayed around home while the boys were usually allowed to wander further afield.

Children playing outside a public house, c. 1895 (Burke). Alcohol played a large part in the lives of many poor children in Liverpool in this period. They often found their way into public houses from a very early age, perhaps to seek one or both parents or to sell newspapers and matches. Sometimes while their parents drank inside, the youngsters would be left to play on the pavement or to be looked after by the eldest child. Laws against children drinking or being in public houses were lax until the 1901 sale of intoxicating drinks to children act.

The terrible effects of excessive drinking and extreme poverty which were to be seen in some areas of Liverpool were described graphically in an article about Scotland Road in the Liverpool Review of 10 November 1883:

We inspected a few houses in the different courts. In one we found a man lying helplessly and speechlessly drunk on a bed of sacks in the parlour. With him was a young woman in a condition of raging delirium. On the step of the house were two little children of about three and four years, clad in nothing but a shirt, and trembling and afraid to enter their home. The woman was tearing round the room as we went in, and protesting that the drunken pig on the bed was "her brother; her lawful brother, and the child of the same parents." This fact or fiction, whichever it may have been, evidently possessed a fascination for the lady, for she never ceased to scream it at the top of her voice during the ten minutes we were in the house. We found that the children were hers, and that they had no place to sleep except the bed where the drunken man was lying, and on which the drunken woman would fling herself when her violence had exhausted itself.

Young boys working on the streets found a variety of ways of earning money — they sold matches and newspapers, helped in markets and carried bags. The youngsters in this photograph, taken by Burke c. 1895 at the Patrick Byrne fountain in Scotland Place at the top of Byrom Street, are shoeblacks.

. busy market scene. One of the pleasanter occupations for a young girl was to work in the market alongside her mother. Other less fortunate
irls traded in the streets selling sundry smallware, matches or chipped wood (Inston).

An article in the Daily Post of 7 November 1883
described some of these basket girls:

The courts in Hodson-street seem largely inhabited by
young girls who earn a precarious living by selling
hips. Further down the street watercress sellers are to
be found. The day our visit was paid was very wet, and
he women had been driven indoors. In one house in
No. 1 Court—a narrow, close nest, with even the
passage blocked up by a door—we found a tiny room
filled full of these chip girls, who sat on the floor, with
a heap of wood before them, chopping away, and
apparently very merry. As may be imagined, the
atmosphere of the place was sickening in the extreme.
These girls have different districts in the town and
outskirts, often walking miles before they reach their
customers. They sell their chips at the rate of a penny
for a dozen bunches, often, however, getting much
less than this. As one girl put it, "Some people is
good, some people is bad; but we 'as to sell the chips
anyway, and we makes generally about tenpence a
day, sometimes as much as a shilling." There are
hundreds of these girls keeping body and soul together
on tenpence a day. Rough creatures as they are, there
is much that is praiseworthy in them. The temptations
to which they are subjected must be very great; the
prospect of release from daily drudgery very alluring.
Yet their worst fault is generally the habit of spending
spare coppers in drink. "Except that," said the
priest, "as a rule they are good girls. They are chiefly
Irish, and Irish girls don't often go wrong."

Boys reading a newspaper outside the Customs House, c. 1890 (Inston). These shoeless street arabs would have been a common sight Liverpool but it is unlikely that many could read. It may be that the boys in the photograph are selling newspapers, a common occupation f boys, although not for girls. A newspaper cart came through the streets and the boys, varying in age from eleven to sixteen, bought a bundle papers, often a dozen or so, for cash with no sale or return agreement. Older boys would be on the streets from 8 a.m. until 10 or 12 p.m although the younger ones would only finish at that late time on Saturdays and would work until 7 or 9 p.m. on weekdays. In July 1878 Mercury reporter described them as '...little half clad children selling papers on doorsteps until 10 or 11 p.m., sometimes asleep in the snow trying to sell the remainder of their bundle of papers.' Newspaper boys earned about 4d. to 5d. an hour and up to 3s. a week if they worked a day Saturday.

Then as now children found great fun in simple things. In this Inston photograph of 1895 a small child is quite happy playing on the streets with his margarine box and his cat.

The Steble Fountain seems to have been a favourite site for many of the children wandering the streets if the youngsters in the two photographs taken by Inston in 1898 are anything to go by. Although all these street urchins are barefoot and scantily clad it was generally considered that Liverpool kept its youngsters reasonably dressed. There existed in the city the Police Aided Clothing Association established in 1895, which helped clothe these children. The antics of such youngsters were not appreciated by all, however, for the Liverpool Courier of 23 June 1906 commented: 'In these times when so much is being done to beautify the centre of the city by means of plants, shrubs and greensward, might it be suggested that something should be done to preserve the beauties of the Steble Fountain from disfigurement by the presence of so many little urchins wading in the cooling waters that descend into the lower basin.'

Above: A scene at St John's Gardens, 1892 (Burke). From their clothes these children are clearly from a much higher social background than those on the opposite page. The boy is wearing an Eton collar and a naval type cap, perhaps because of the naval exhibition advertised on the railings of the Walker Art Gallery in the background. The girls are wearing heavy dresses, cloaks and bonnets.

A game of 'jacks', Richmond Row, c. 1900 (Burke).

Above left: Bathing in the Leeds Liverpool canal by Burlington Street Bridge, c. 1900 (Inston). These lads are enjoying a bathe locally where bathing suits were not a 'must', although in the presence of the photographer a sense of modesty prevails.

Below left: This splendid studio photograph taken in June 1899 on the Isle of Man was found in a Liverpool shop. It is probable that the two in the photograph were from Liverpool on a day outing or a longer holiday to the Isle of Man. Obviously the photograph was taken on the son's behalf. His mother does not seem too pleased about it all.

Catching tiddlers by Canal Bridge, Lightbody Street. The water had a fascinating attraction for boys, be it by the docks or by the canal, as in this photograph taken by Inston about 1890. Notice the bare feet and caps. Other pastimes for boys included football, pitch and toss, marbles and fighting! Children could invent games and interests and make up songs and rhymes, whatever the surroundings.

...ldren playing outside a general store in Richmond Row, c 1895 (Burke). Skipping was a favourite pastime of girls in this period, especially of ...se living in cobbled streets because of the impressive noise of the rope hitting the stones. Girls also played with dolls or at hop-scotch. In the ...tograph one of the girls wears a shawl, as her mother would have done, and the little boy sports a cap, ever popular with young and old.

The brigantine 'Guitar', 1891.

Riverside

The basis of Liverpool's prosperity was her port and shipping. In 1800 474 vessels entered the port, averaging ninety-four tons, while in 1908 there were 25,739, averaging 665 tons. The impact of this growth on Liverpool was aptly described by the Victorian novelist Albert Smith with the words 'ships, ships and shipping everywhere'. The photographs in this chapter, taken mainly between 1880 and 1912, allow us an impressive glimpse of the ships, the docks and, of course, the Mersey.

Until the 1870s the sailing ship remained t chief form of water transport. Steam driven sh had appeared in the first decades of the nir teenth century but it was not until importa technological developments had occurred in t 1850s and 1860s that the steamship gained decided advantage over the sailing ship. By t mid 1870s more steamships than sailing shi were being built annually in the United Kir dom, and thereafter the trend accelerated.

Although by 1880 the steamship had becor

re important than the sailing ship, there were l many sailing ships to be seen on the Mersey, ging from large four masted clippers to much aller vessels such as schooners. While the amers had taken over most of the Atlantic and senger trade by the 1880s, the sailing ships l played a very important role in the Australian l South American trade, as well as in the local stal trade. In face of increasing numbers of amships this role declined, however, and by First World War sailing ships were of little nmercial importance.

The size and speed of steamships increased matically. By 1874 there were ships of over 00 tons crossing the Atlantic in seven days, while by 1894 ships of 13,000 tons were crossing in five days. On the eve of the First World War the largest ships were over 50,000 tons, capable of a transatlantic crossing in five days.

Many shipping lines had offices in Liverpool. Some of these companies had commenced business from Liverpool and by the late nineteenth century had become major world shipping lines, such as Cunard and White Star.

The photographer who best captured this aspect of Liverpool life was Arthur Priestley who ran a commercial photographic business at Egremont from the 1880s until the 1930s. He was an official photographer for Cunard.

ough this poster is dated slightly before our period it has been included because it is a good example of a Liverpool shipping poster and is for company on which the television series, the Onedin Line, was based.

Prince's landing stage, September 1896. In this picture of a busy riverside can be seen many of the different types of boats on the Mersey.
front ship in line is a paddle steamer tug, followed by a steamer and a White Star tender. Behind these can be seen a square rigged steam s.
paddle steam ferry boats and sailing trawlers.

hn Masefield spent part of his youth, from 1891 to *94, as a cadet on the training ship 'Conway' which *s moored in the Mersey. In his writings he made *ny references to this period of his life and the sights *hich had so fascinated him while living on the *onway'. His poems connected with Liverpool *clude 'The Wanderer' and 'Liverpool, 1890'. The *llowing extract from his history of the 'Conway' *ves an appealing picture of the bustling ship life to *e seen on the Mersey in the last decade of the *neteenth century.*

*rty years ago the flower of all England's shipping *longed in Liverpool: the river and docks were always *sy with the best ships of the time. The Cunard *oorings were just downstream from us; the White *ar and Inman moorings beyond them; the P.S.N. *d Alfred Holt moorings still further on, but in *ght. The Elder Dempster ships were near us in the *oyne. The steamers of many famous lines were *ekly visitors to the river, we knew them all, their *nnels, their house-flags and their tenders: even the *reign steamers and what they brought were known *us.

But in those days the bulk of the world's freight was *rried in sailing ships, which had then reached their *st, strange, beautiful perfection. At all times we *uld see in the river or in the docks the queens of *at last construction, the superb four-masted ships *d barques, of from two to three thousand tons, *hich went with general cargoes to San Francisco and *me back with grain. They are now gone, but then *ey were many; and many of the many were strange *th new device of build or rig, of intense interest to *, whose talk and thought was of ships.

At flood tide in any case the river would waken into *stle and beauty of ships coming in and going out, *l it would seem like a street with ships for people.

The dock-gates would open to the sound of cheers to let pass some ship with her blue peter flying; barges would tack by under their red sails; schooners, brigantines, yawls and ketches went out or returned, under all sail. Greek and Italian polaccas of all sizes came in under sail. Norwegian barques sometimes sailed in, tack and tack, to anchor near us. No such display of living ships could be seen in any other port in the world at that time.

The display did not cease with the living ships, far from it. On both sides of the river there were the slips and gantries of the building firms, and all the racket and clatter of new construction, always going on in sight and sound of us. We watched ships being built and launched and floated. We saw them going forth in splendour and coming back shattered by the sea, listed, shored up, dismasted, red with sea-rust, white with sea-salt, holed, dinted, ruined, all pumps still spouting, just limping into dock with three tugs, or just crawling to the mud and lying down.

And with these, we saw the ships of the river services; not only the tugs, famous all over the world, such as the *Helen Dagmar*, the *Blazer*, the *Kings* and the *Cocks*, but the ferries and the bar-dredgers, the salvage and diving craft; all the fleet of a great port.

For beauty, interest and variety no scene on earth could compare with the river in which we lived. We were in the sea-world and of it, initiated into the mystery and free of the guild, and there at its busiest heart. Of all the many joys that youth and the ship offered, that gift of beauty was the greatest.

Looking out on those scenes as we did, even the dullest of us said, in the words of our grace: "For these and all His mercies the Lord's Name be praised."

The Conway: from her foundation to the present day (London, 1933), pp 119-21.

The 'Parthenope' was among the fastest and most comfortable clippers on the Australian run. In 1876 one of the first class passengers aboard ship was J. J. Williams of Bangor, North Wales, and from his letters written on the journey we can discover something of what life was like on these ships for passengers and crew.

Ship *Parthenope*
Lat. 41 deg. 0 min. S.
Long. 6 deg. 36 min. E.

September 14, 1876

I regret very much that I have not had an opportunity of sending you any letters home by passing ships, and I am almost certain that between this and Melbourne we shall not see any homeward-bound ships as they all sail in another direction. We have been spoken several times by homeward-bound ships, but it has always happened that at the time it was either blowing too hard, with heavy seas running, or the distance between us was too great to pass letters. However, I hope that our ship has been reported several times in the newspapers. Our captain took great pains in signalling and in every case requested that we should be reported "all well."

Up to the present time we have not made any extraordinary time, and if the future and latter end of the voyage is as slow as the former part we shall have made rather a long passage for a clipper ship, but of course we must take the wind and weather as we find them — we have this much consolation, we have passed every ship we have been in company with, and some of those, the very fastest ships afloat and noted for their sailing capabilities.

Before I go any further I think I had better describe the ship, crew and passengers. I am glad to report that I have been exceedingly fortunate in the choice of my ship. The *Parthenope* is one of the most sea-worthy ships afloat, being a new ship, on her second voyage. All the tackle and gear are of the very best, and there is plenty of everything in the shape of spare materials and extra stores; all the sails are new this voyage, and it is a comfort to think in a gale of wind that every-thing aloft is quite secure, and not in danger of carrying away.

The crew numbers the captain, first, second an third officers, carpenter, sailmaker, engineer, painte 20 A.B.s and ordinary seamen, boatswain, fo quartermasters, chief steward, assistant steward (s loon), second cabin steward, cook, cook's mate, fi apprentices and three stowaways, making a total of 4(Four saloon passengers and 25 second cabin an steerage passengers make a grand total of 75 souls o board.

We have very good living on board, the saloon tabl being supplied with livestock and poultry. We had 1 sheep and 15 pigs starting from Liverpool and abou six dozen ducks and chickens. There is a good suppl of fresh meat at every meal; we kill one sheep and pig every week which, when jointed, come upon th saloon table. What is left goes to the apprentice. The second and steerage passengers get no fowl (fresh meat; they are fed with tinned meats.

The sailors do not receive a drop of liquor, but the is always plenty of hot coffee for them day and nigh and the captain says he never gives men anything bu coffee on the most stormy of winter nights, nor do he take anything himself. The men, on the oth hand, don't want drink at sea, they prefer coffee, bu I assure you they drink a very large quantity of it an it is a very expensive business for the owners to keep teetotal ship.

Up to the present time I have enjoyed the voyag very much and the sea agrees with me. I have seen great many wonders that are connected with a sailor life, but I must say it is a very hard one indeed and would not advise any lad to go to sea that can g anything at all to do ashore. Poor boys! They get hard time of it at sea. In this ship the boys get bett times and better food than in most others, but what is to be on board one of those old wooden, half-rotte ships that Mr. Plimsoll is putting down, I cannot sa but I imagine it is something fearful.

I would not be a sailor for a mine of gold, but to g as a passenger on board a fine ship like this is one (the most enjoyable and interesting experiences and would advise anyone with time and money to spare (c if business calls for it) to take a sea voyage.

from 'First class passage in sail' in *Sea Breezes* XV
1953, pp 392-8

The clipper 'Parthenope' in the Queen's graving dock, May 1895. Built by Evans of Liverpool and owned by the local shipping company, Gracie, Beasley and Co., the 'Parthenope' was a very fast iron sailing ship of 1646 tons, engaged principally in the Australian trade, carrying emigrants and manufactured goods on the outward trip and wool on the return journey. The 'Parthenope' made the Australian trip regularly in under eighty days. She went missing in 1907 off New South Wales.

The barque 'Charlwood', n.d. Built in 1877 at Sunderland and owned by another small local company, G. H. Fletcher and Co., she was employed in a variety of foreign trade.

Prince's dock, 1891. The barrels on the dockside were used for shipping various products, one of the most important being rum.

The Albert dock, 1895. Designed by Tesse Hortley and opened in 1840, it was important because it was the first to incorporate an enclosed system of warehousing.

Queen's and Coburg docks, 1895. The square rigged sailing ships seen here were engaged in deep water trade.

e docks were usually scenes of great activity. rman Melville, author of Moby Dick, *visited Liver- ol a number of times. In his book* Redburn *he gives gthy descriptions of life on the Liverpool water- nt. The following description from* Redburn *was itten in 1849 but the picture he draws is valid also the later dock scenes shown on these two pages.*

rounded by its broad belt of masonry, each Liver- ol dock is a walled town, full of life and com- tion; or rather, is a small archipelago, an epitome the world, where all the nations of Christendom, even those of Heathendom, are represented. For, tself, each ship is an island, a floating colony of the e to which it belongs.

Here are brought together the remotest limits of the th; and in the collective spars and timbers of these s, all the forests of the globe are represented, as in and parliament of masts. Canada and New Zea- d send their pines; America her live oak; India her ; Norway her spruce; and the Right Honourable hogany, member for Honduras and Campeachy, is at his post by the wheel.

A Liverpool dock is a grand caravansary inn, and l, on the spacious and liberal plan of the *Astor* use. Here ships are lodged at a moderate charge, payment is not demanded till the time of

departure. Here they are comfortably housed and provided for; sheltered from all weathers and secured from all calamities.

I know not how many hours I spent in gazing at the shipping in Prince's Dock, and speculating concerning their past voyages and future prospects in life. Some had just arrived from the most distant ports, worn, battered, and disabled; others were all a-taunt-o— spruce, gay, and brilliant, in readiness for sea.

Every day the Highlander had some new neighbour. A black brig from Glasgow, with its crew of sober Scotch caps, and its staid, thrifty-looking skipper, would be replaced by a jovial French hermaphrodite, its forecastle echoing with songs, and its quarter-deck elastic from much dancing.

On the other side, perhaps, a magnificent New York Liner, huge as a seventy-four, and suggesting the idea of a Mivart's or Delmonico's afloat, would give way to a Sidney emigrant ship, receiving on board its live freight of shepherds from the Grampians, ere long to be tending their flocks on the hills and downs of New Holland.

from Redburn: his first voyage; being the sailor-boy confessions and reminiscences of the son-of-a-gentle- man, in the merchant service. *(New York, 1849; new impression, London, 1925) pp 165-6.*

GREAT EASTERN P.W.S. 2165.

Above: The 'Great Eastern', photographed here in 1888 following her beaching at New Ferry, was a ship of revolutionary design which stron influenced the development of the steamship. She was five times the size of the biggest ship afloat at her launching in 1858 and had m special features. One of these was the three different means of propulsion — paddle wheels, a screw propeller and sails. In spite of her techn achievements, and her great size and speed, the ship was a commercial failure, largely through financial mismanagement.

Above right: The S.S. 'Cufic' being towed by tender, 1898. Both ships were owned by the White Star line and built in Belfast, as were most the White Star ships. The 'Cufic', which was built in 1888, was the first of the White Star's livestock carriers. She was sold in 1901 to Dominion line and again in 1915 to a Canadian line. She sank in the North Atlantic in 1919. The tender is probably the 'Magnetic' wh transferred passengers to and from the company's liners anchored in the Mersey and which sometimes towed ships. As her flag of destinat shows, the 'Cufic' was on her way to the United States when this photograph was taken.

Below right: The S.S. 'Dakar', May 1909. Owned by Elder Dempster, this ship was engaged mainly on the West African run, carryt passengers and cargo. The most common type of cargo was bananas. In the background can be seen the Liver Buildings in the process construction.

The S.S. 'Lucania', seen through the chains for the ferry landing stage extension at Egremont, 1894. The 'Lucania' was the fastest transatlan... liner at the time that this photograph was taken. On her maiden voyage in September 1893, she crossed the Atlantic in five days, fifteen hour... within a short time this was reduced by over seven hours.

...ers of the 1890s such as the 'Lucania' were truly, as ...eir brochures proclaimed, stately homes at sea. Their ...xurious fittings contrasted sharply with the primitive ...rnishings and conditions of ships of a short time ...eviously. Sir W. R. Forwood, a prominent Liverpool ...ipowner, described graphically these earlier con-...tions in his memoirs.

...ose who travelled across the Atlantic in the early ...ties will recall the stuffy passenger saloons, placed ...ht aft, with no seats except the long settees, and lit ...ly by candles suspended on trays, which swayed to ...d fro sputtering grease right and left. The state-...oms were placed below the saloon and were lit by oil ...nps, one between every two rooms. These were ...igiously put out at ten o'clock every night.

There was no ventilation, and no hot water was ...tainable. We have always thought that the intro-...ction of the electric light was a greater boon, and ...ore appreciated on board ship than anywhere else. ...a rough, wild night, when everything in your state-...om is flying about, and you begin to conjure up ...oughts of possible disaster, if you switch on the ...ctric light, all is at peace. The very waves appear to ...robbed of their fury. There were no smoke-rooms ...the olden days—the lee side of the funnel in fine ...ather, the fiddlee at other times. Here, seated on ...ls of rope, and ready to lift our feet as the seas ...led in from the alleyways on either side, we smoked ...d spun our yarns. There was an abundance of food ...the saloon in the shape of great huge joints of meat ...d dishes of vegetables, which were placed on the ...ble, and it required some gymnastic agility to be ...dy to seize them, when the ship gave a lurch, to ...event their being deposited on your lap. We had no ...viettes, but there came the enormous compensation ...: all deficiencies—it was deftly whispered, "the ...nard never lost a life," and not another word was ...d.

The conditions of life in the steerage were wretched.

The sleeping berths were huddled together, neces-sitating the occupants climbing over each other; there was no privacy, no washing accommodation except at the common tap, no saloon or seating accommodation except on the hatchways. The food was brought round in iron buckets, and junks of beef and pork were forked out by the steward, and placed in the pas-senger's pannikin, and in a similar way potatoes and plum duff were served out.

All this has been changed, and in place of discom-fort we have luxurious accommodation for every class of traveller.

from Sir W. R. Forwood, *Reminiscences of a ship-owner* (Liverpool, 1920 pp 31-3.

By the 1890s passengers travelled in style. The 'Lucania', built in 1893 for Cunard, offered spacious lounges, reading rooms and saloons, with wooden panelling, open coal fires and electric light. She kept six bakers, four butchers and three confectioners con-stantly at work preparing food. In the saloon gallery were cooking stoves twenty-five feet long, by four feet wide. Conditions had also improved greatly for second and third class passengers who were provided with berth cabins of various sizes. The number of passen-gers carried was approximately 450 in the first, 300 in the second and 700 in the third class or steerage; the crew numbered about 400.

Various first class interiors in transatlantic liners in the 1890s: above, dining saloon on the S.S. 'Lucania', 1894; above right, library on R.M.S. 'Cymric', 1899; below right, drawing room on the S.S. 'Campania', n.d.

Liverpool street scene, c. 1895 (Inston). This character study captures much of the lively atmosphere of the city's back streets.

Street scenes

Guide books of late nineteenth century Liverpool directed visitors to the city's principal streets and buildings, such as those recorded by Francis Frith. This view of Liverpool, however, is not a complete one, for then, as today, the atmosphere of Liverpool life cannot be appreciated without wandering away from the main thoroughfares towards intriguing back streets, market places and alleyways. Fortunately for us this side of Liverpool life was captured in the photographs of Thomas Burke and C. F. Inston, both of whom were more concerned with portraying people than places in their work.

They photographed a world of impromptu markets, perpetual barrow boys and women gossiping at street corners. In this world children were always on the streets selling oddments from hatguards to matches, and the beggars and tramps were familiar sights to all. Familiar, too, were the policemen, or 'scuffers', and, in the less salubrious parts of town, the drunks and the prostitutes. It would not have been difficult for Burke or Inston to find groups of men without employment, or hordes of truant children to photograph. Through their work we can catch a glimpse of the more colourful side of Liverpool street life which would have been so familiar to city dwellers at the end of the nineteenth century.

...shwives outside the market at Great ...harlotte Street, photographed by Inston, ...890.

Markets were an integral part of this Liverpool ...reet life. They varied from groups of women ...lling their rags or wood chips on the pavements ... corporation controlled markets. By 1900 there ...ere six of these, some wholesale, others retail. St ...ohn's market, prominently situated near the ...ntre of the city, was the principal market for ...e public. Here fruit, meat, poultry and garden ...roduce were sold, and spaces were reserved for ...rmers who attended on Saturday to sell their ...roduce. Connected to St John's were two ...ncovered markets, one for the sale of poultry ...d live birds and the other for the sale of ...dlars' wares, while nearby was a fish market.

For the ordinary man or woman in late ...ictorian Liverpool there were many different ...pes of entertainment. Besides the colourful ...eryday scenes and events which were free for ...l, there existed music halls such as the Old Star, ...ax work shows, theatres and visiting circuses and ...irs. Soccer was becoming popular for partici-...ants and spectators alike; both Liverpool and ...verton football teams originated in 1878. Horse ...cing, hare coursing and boxing were also much ...njoyed. Public houses provided another form of ...opular and cheap entertainment, mainly for

men. While the musical tastes of the upper and middle classes were catered for at the Philhar-monic Hall, the masses had the pleasure of hearing the sounds of the many brass and silver bands to be found in the city. The pleasant parks around the city provided places of quiet and beauty for many. Cheap day excursions to Egremont, New Brighton and the Isle of Man were another source of popular enjoyment.

In spite of this variety of amusements life was still harsh for the poor and it took more than a stroll along the docks to forget their problems. Much of the employment in the city was on a casual basis, especially in the docks where the main source of employment for Liverpool's male population was to be found. In spite of growing trade union activity in the late nineteenth century pay was frequently low and conditions could be extremely harsh — a working man's or woman's escape from dire poverty frequently lay only in the form of alcohol. Oftentimes people wandered the streets because they had nothing else to do. At the same time, as these photographs clearly show, people put a cheerful face on things and endeavoured to cope with life as best they could.

Owen Campbell's marine and general store at No. 28 Athol Street, c. 1905 (Inston). The owner is taking full advantage of the space afforded by the pavement to advertise his goods to passers by.

This scene of an accident involving a horse and cart of the London and North Western Railway Company has captured the attention of many curious bystanders. It was taken in South John Street by Inston in 1890.

An interesting Liverpool street scene showing the old Adelphi Hotel with a row of hansom cabs in the foreground, taken in 1900 by Burke. The comings and goings of its many guests from all over the world would often cause great excitement in the city. This majestic hotel — Dickens thought it was the best in the world — was owned by the Midland Railway Company and built in the years 1868-9 on the site of the White House Tavern which at one time was linked with the Ranelagh Gardens, a popular entertainments area. It contained nearly three hundred bedrooms and fifty parlours, together with elegant drawing, smoking and grand banqueting rooms. In 1912 this hotel was demolished and replaced by the now familiar Adelphi designed by Frank Atkinson.

The Adelphi's reputation for turtle soup was second to none. The hotel's guide book from the late nineteenth century mentioned that in the basement could be found:

'...an institution quite unique in Liverpool and with few parallels in the United Kingdom. It is a tank in which the turtles are kept until required for use in the establishment. Between 60 and 70 of these expensive and delicious monsters may at times be seen swimming comfortably in their tank, little conscious of the glorious fate that awaits them.'

This photograph of women selling clothes was taken by Burke in 1895 in the vicinity of Paddy's market. The market was as famous then as it is now. People from all over Liverpool and all manner and type of sailors and visitors from further afield frequented the market.

The following extract from the Daily Post *of 8 November 1883 gives us a colourful picture of the bustling market activity:*

At the top of Banastre-street a spectacle is to be witnessed which cannot be seen anywhere else in Liverpool. It is a striking example of trade in its most rudimentary form. Here is held what is known as ''Paddy's Market.'' Inside this place, about three o'clock in the afternoon, you may see a most extraordinary gathering of tattered humanity. The place is densely crowded by a shouting, gesticulating, swearing, and generally animated mob. Buyers and sellers are nearly all women, and the articles bought and sold appear to be mainly rags. The vendors squat behind heaps of rubbish, which you would not touch with a stick, and passing in front, turning over the mass, criticising, cheapening, consulting with friends, and purchasing, are swarms of matrons enjoying the whole business, just after the fashion of ladies shopping in Bold-street.

Poultry market at Upper Dawson Street, c. 1890 (Inston).

reat Charlotte Street, here photographed
Inston in 1890, ran from Old
ymarket to Ranelagh Street and con-
ned three markets, two of which sold
h while the other sold fruit, flowers,
ovisions and meat.

e whole street was almost always busy
th its pavements frequently obstructed
boxes, baskets and crates from the
rious markets. The horse-drawn carts,
den with goods, also blocked the way for
yone wanting to walk around. The
unger basket girls here were, it seems, in
e habit of daubing fish on the dresses of
e ladies entering the covered market. It
s these shoeless maidens who, the Liver-
ol Review stated in April 1899, had a
cabulary 'enriched by a supple lexicon of
rid expletives' which they used 'extra-
gantly and freely upon passers by'. The
icle continued: 'The road and pavement
re often present to the pedestrians' gaze
mixed mass of oyster shells, smashed fish,
weeds and cods' heads, which, with
my eyes, gaze up pathetically at the dis-
sted wayfarer as he gingerly picks his way
ongst them.'

it vendor at the Old Haymarket, c.
0 (Inston).

Onlookers at Mann Island stall, c. 1895 (Inston). Mann Island, as it was in the late nineteenth century, was a small island which lay at the si[de] of the old George's dock, connected to the waterfront by means of a steel bridge. It is said that true scousers, or Dicky Sams, have to be bo[rn] within a mile from this place. The island, notorious for its number of pubs, was the favourite haunt of many sailors and dockers.

Animals were a common sight at Pier Head, as can be seen from these two photographs taken by Inston around 1890. The photograph bel[ow] right shows sheep gathered at St Nicholas' Place; they are probably coming off one of the ferry boats. On the right are work horses enjoying a w[ell] earned rest on the floating bridge. It is likely that they were used to pull trams or heavy vehicles of the type used around the docks. When th[e] photograph was taken horses played a vital role in the city's transport — the horse tram era did not end finally until 1903. The men who look[ed] after these horses often had an intense pride in their animals, and in the May day parades many of them were exquisitely groomed a[nd] exhibited.

Men outside the Customs House, c. 189[...]
This is one of many Inston photograp[...]
portraying groups of men standing arour[...]
Liverpool smoking their clay pipes. I[...]
evitable hardship lies behind the stol[...]
faces and aggressive stances. The possibili[...]
of being without work was ever present fe[...]
many, especially as dock work fluctuated [...]
much due to the ebbs and flows of trad[...]
At this time there was no dole or soci[...]
security to rely on, and for the tru[...]
destitute the workhouse provided the on[...]
relief, as outdoor relief had been abar[...]
doned earlier in the century. The indiv[...]
dual could lean on charities or philan[...]
thropic persons such as Father Nugent [...]
David Lewis for comfort, if not for finance[...]
Old age pensions were not introduced unt[...]
1908 and it was not until 1912 tha[...]
schemes were established for unemploy[...]
ment or health insurance. Althoug[...]
income was irregular for the male of th[...]
household, his wife could often find wor[...]
in the tailoring industry, in the markets [...]
else as a shoemaker, domestic servant[...]
bookbinder or laundress. Alternatively, sh[...]
could become the neighbourhood washer[...]
woman or money-lender. Children wer[...]
begging or selling on the streets at an earl[...]
age. For the old the solution was not eas[...]
as few families could afford to suppor[...]
their elderly relatives. Again the city[...]
workhouses — the biggest in England —[...]
or charity homes often provided the answe[...]

Women standing at a street corner, c 1895[...]
(Burke). It is impossible to guess the ages[...]
of many of these women as the hardships[...]
that they and others like them experienced[...]
took heavy toll on their appearance and[...]
personality. In the poorer quarters the[...]
married women's battle against poverty[...]
was harsh and unceasing.

n interesting insight into their lives and conditions
n be found in a report of 1911 into the domestic
rroundings of Liverpool's casual labourers.

wing to the strong breeze that blows up from the
ver, the poor quarters of Liverpool, with the excep-
on of court and cellar dwellings, do not suffer from
uffiness as much, perhaps, as those of other towns.
he winds, however, bring the disadvantage that the
irt which lies in the imperfectly scavenged streets is
uickly dried and blown down the throat and nostrils
f the passer-by and into the houses. The want of
roper back-premises and of space and arrangements
r washing in many of the houses is another impedi-
ent to cleanliness. Yet another, as the study of the
udgets in detail reminds one, is the cost of soap,
lacklead, brushes, etc. When the income is in-
ufficient for necessary food, it is not perhaps sur-
rising that the 3d. to 6d. per week, which seems
out the sum usually spent in the better kept homes
n cleaning materials, is the first item to be cut down
y the less particular housewives.

The instinct of housepride seems almost never en-
rely wanting, at least in the homes studied. Some
tempt at ornament is always made, and coloured
rints, photographs and dust-collecting knicknacks
ten abound in homes from which the more pawn-
le articles of useful furniture have been stripped.

Of the family life led in these homes, the enquiry
ve only occasional glimpses, sometimes cheerful and
metimes deeply depressing. At one moment one is
ruck by how independent affection can be of cir-
mstance, as exemplified by the many proud and
fectionate mothers of sickly, unattractive children, or
y the daughter of the house in budget No. 16, who
hen removed to a situation from the eleventh share
the family cellar and bread and tea, wept and
lked till a place close to "home" was found for her.
t another, the prevalent impression left is that when
e struggle for existence is at its hardest, emotion
ly lasts till it has accomplished the primary end for
hich Nature intended it, marital feeling only till
ildbearing has become a certainty, parental feeling
ly while the youth of the children makes parental

care a necessity. The perfectly dispassionate frankness
with which husbands are discussed and marriage
admitted a failure, the absence of any sign of feeling
in announcing and describing a death in the family,
may sometimes be deceptive. The ignorance frequently
displayed of the whereabouts of any of several married
sons and daughters, especially sons, supposed to be
living in the same town, but whom "we haven't seen
nothing of for years," is occasionally put on to baffle
enquirers. Often, however, these things seem plainly
the outcome of a vitality so lowered and deadened by
privation and toil that it is unequal to any effort
beyond that of meeting the elementary needs of
physical life. Healthy and well-to-do people will
understand the phenomena better if they remember
the kind of paralysis of the affections and the will that
has sometimes fallen on themselves in sea-sickness or
nervous headache, or when excessively run down. The
facial expression and carriage of many of the poorer
working women in and after middle life (*i.e.*, in that
class, from about 30 onwards), suggest that their
condition is one of chronic suffering, so habitual that
they are scarcely conscious of it, due to extreme
anaemia, weariness, and the various small ailments
that result from self-neglect, over-exertion and under-
nourishment, during the years of childbearing. On the
whole one is more astonished at the amount some of
them accomplish in their homes with so poor an
equipment, and at the high level of devotion, patience
and cheerfulness they reach, than at the deficiencies of
others.

How the casual labourer lives: report of the Liver-
pool joint research committee on the domestic con-
dition and expenditure of the families of certain
Liverpool labourers.

(Liverpool, 1909) pp 23-24

A three horse tram on Mann Island, c. 1890 (Inston). Conditions of work for tramway employees were harsh in this period. In 1889 a union,
Liverpool Amalgamated Tramway and Hackney Carriage Employees Association, was formed to obtain better terms for tramway workers.
campaign was organised to protest about conditions but this collapsed in a short time and the union failed to get recognition, thus leading to
demise. Not until the early twentieth century did an effective trade union organise the tramway employees. Other unions were more success
and their activity among various types of workers such as seamen and gas workers grew rapidly from the 1880s onwards.

...wnpour at Pier Head, c. 1890 (Inston).

The Cork steamer discharging cattle, February 1901, at the Prince's landing stage. The import of cattle from Ireland was an important busin *in this period. The cattle were driven from the landing stage through the streets to the cattle market, a distance of about three miles.*

Docks and Dockers

'The dock system on both sides of the Mersey — Liverpool and Birkenhead — is the finest in the world, and accounts in a year for imports and exports of the value of about £300,000,000. Upon the docks and their working, the prosperity of Liverpool, and indeed, of Lancashire and great part of the kingdom, mainly depends.'

A pictorial and descriptive guide to Liverpoo Birkenhead, New Brighton, the Wirral, et (London, 1912, eleventh edition), p. 10

During the nineteenth and early twentieth centuries, the growth in Liverpool's trade and the number of ships using the port led to constantly increasing demands on her port facilities. In 1800 the tonnage of ships entering and leaving the port was under half a million while in 1900 it was twelve million and in 1914 it had grown to nineteen million. To cope with this growing trade, the docks were expanded and improved, and to deal with the increasing size of ships, especially from the 1860s, due to rapid increase in the size of steamships, radical changes in the design and equipment of the docks were introduced.

Of prime importance in this development was the establishment in 1857 of the Mersey Docks and Harbour Board which took over complete control of port facilities at Liverpool and Birkenhead. The board ran the docks very effectively, supervising an ambitious investment policy which allowed the port to keep apace with the growing trade. The photographs in this chapter were taken by an unknown photographer who was employed by the board to record some of the work in progress in the docks around the turn of the century.

By 1900 the docks stretched about seven and a quarter miles on the Liverpool side of the Mersey from the Herculaneum dock at the south end to the Hornby dock at the north. This vast system of docks provided accomodation for all types of vessels, from the largest liners of the day to small coastal boats. The quays were well equipped with various appliances and cranes which allowed the efficient handling of goods, while rail connections between the quays and the main railway lines allowed swift movement of passenger and goods traffic. There were vast warehouses for all sorts of goods. Graving docks were available for the repair and servicing of ships. On the Birkenhead side an extensive dock system was also developed.

The docks were the main source of employment in Liverpool. There was a great variety of occupations to be found on the waterfront, including carters, warehouse workers and dock labourers. It has been estimated that at the end of the nineteenth century about 25,000 men were employed on the dock estate at any given time. Trade unions had appeared as far back as the 1840s but the movement became a serious factor in the docks only in the early 1890s. The National Union of Dock Labourers was formed in 1889 and by 1891 it had five branches in Liverpool.

Dock labourers were the most numerous group of workers in the docks and almost without exception they were employed on a casual basis. This system of casual employment had harsh consequences for those involved as work was never certain from day to day and was subject to influences of trade and weather. In 1912 a clearing house system for the registration and employment of dock labourers was introduced but it was not until 1967 that the casual system was finally abolished.

Ship unloading cargo at the north shed of the Queen's Branch Dock, West End, February 1903. This dock was used mainly by ships in the Spanish and East Indian trade.

Dock labourers, the largest group of workers in the docks, were not employed as general labourers but carried out specialised jobs. The principal types of dock labourers' jobs were well described in an article in the Liverpool Citizen, *16 July 1890.*

It is astonishing how little acquainted the ordinary Liverpool citizen is with the varied and intricate operations performed by those ''working at the docks.'' In the seeming confusion and bustle there is an underlying discipline and order—the outgrowth of hard, practical experience in obtaining the greatest possible results with the minimum waste of time and power. When trade is brisk it is a question if a busier scene could anywhere be found than the Liverpool docks present, and perhaps in no part of the world are human sinew and muscle more effectively exerted.

If we exclude those who follow regular lines of employment, such as riggers, coal and salt heavers,

&c., we find the great army of dock labourers engaged in loading and discharging ships. To the ordinary citizen these may appear simple enough; their proper performance requires a combination of skill, tact, and judgment. The work is in the hands of three distinct classes of labourers—stevedores, lumpers, and porters, whose lines of labour are as distinctly marked as are the official jobs of the naval, military, and civil services.

The stevedore's duty is to ship and stow the goods forming the cargo; the lumper unstows and unships the cargo; the porter receives it at the ship's side, weighs it, assorts it according to its lots or marks, stows it on the quay, and loads it off. It will thus be seen that the stevedore deals alone with outward cargo, the lumper and porter with inward. The difficulties of the stevedore may be judged by anyone passing a berth where cargo is arriving for shipment. Rails, railway engines, tenders, carriages, bridges, columns, man

62

inery of every shape, size, and weight, machines of
most complicated and delicate workmanship,
ckages and bales of fine and valuable goods, casks of
and of liquids of every description—these have to
stowed in the ship's hold so that, no matter how
may be tossed by wind or wave, there must be no
ifting; the fine goods must be so placed that they
stain no damage from any injurious cargo being
owed over or around them, and all must be so
sposed that the vessel sits in a trim and shipshape
hion. The vessel, too, may be—usually is—bound
r many different ports, necessitating an arrangement
the cargo so that the consignment for each port can
landed expeditiously (time is money to the ship-
ner or charterer), and without interfering with the
ssel's seaworthiness to proceed on her voyage. The
xterity displayed in lifting, shipping, and stowing
ticles of several tons weight, and of every conceivable
ape, is something marvellous. The ablest professor
physical science would make a poor show in a test of
actical application of the mechanical powers with the
dinary labouring stevedore.

The lumper's title is evidently derived from the
ugh-and-ready way in which a bargain was struck
tween the consignee of the cargo and the person
dertaking the unshipment in years past. A *lump*
m was agreed on for the performance of that labour.
e "breaking out" of the goods in the hold is a work
the greatest nicety and difficulty. Cotton, for
stance, is so tightly screwed into the hold that the
ip's sides are often strained. The lumper's man has
adjust the gearing, set the booms, fix the pulleys or
gins," arrange the "falls" or ropes of the pulley,
d load the slings in which the articles are secured for
isting. In addition, he has to arrange stages, detach
e slings, and pass the goods on to the quay or over
e sides to another vessel. He must be agile aloft as a
ilor, while he has to delve below with the persistence
d force of a navvy.

The porter receives the cargo at the ship's side. The
nding clerk is supplied with a "manifest," a docu-
ent containing an abstract of the cargo, each con-
gnment separately set out with its distinctive mark,
ually a combination of three or four letters, some-
mes placed in a triangle or other plain figure, and
ten accompanied by, say, a representation of a dart,
heart, or a crown, &c. On the manifest each consign-

ment or "lot" has its lot number. These generally run
consecutively. To give an idea of the porter's manner
of working we may assume the case of a cargo of
American cotton, comprising ten or twelve thousand
bales, divided into a hundred lots. The number in the
lots varies considerably. When the lumper delivers the
bale at the ship's side, the porters place it in the scales
to be weighed. A man stands on each side of the scale
provided with an ink-pot and a brush. One of them
(the "lotter") notes the mark on the bale, casts his eye
down the manifest till he finds the mark there, sees
the lot number, which he paints on the bale, while his
companion puts on the weight the weigher calls out,
and is jointly responsible with him for its accuracy.
The bale is then placed on a truck, the trucker keeping
watch for the lot number, which he calls out after
clearing from the scales, and he is immediately
directed to the quarter of the quay assigned to the
sub-division of the cargo...

This short notice may show the reader that even
dock work can scarcely be put down as unskilled
labour. The employers well know the advantages of
having old hands "on the job," though recent events
might seem to contradict this statement. Strength and
will would naturally appear to be the only requisites
for that simple form of labour, bag-carrying. There are
men at the docks who would freely make a substantial
wager that they could find two men on the quay,
under ten-stone weight, who would soon leave Samson
and Sandow nowhere in a job of bag-carrying. It is by
no means unusual to see strong, healthy-looking men
of fourteen or fifteen stone weight dropping out of
gangs of bag-carriers, exhausted, about ten or eleven
o'clock in the forenoon; while men of not seemingly
over nine stone would gamely continue carrying till
five p.m., and often anxiously inquire if there was a
chance of the ship working till night. With a pretty
extensive knowledge of the British Islands, and from
inquiries made of observant persons who have visited
other lands, this statement may be risked with con-
fidence—That in no part of the world is there com-
paratively more real hard work performed, or where
men with equal determination or power of physical
endurance can be found to attempt its performance,
than is accomplished in Liverpool by men who get a
precarious existence "working at the docks."

64

ve left: Ground floor of a double storey shed at the Huskisson Branch Dock, no. 1., in May 1902, showing an inward cargo consisting of rent foodstuffs. This was part of the Canada-Huskisson system which had the best accommodation for vessels in Liverpool at this time,

w left: Testing a new concrete floor in the Coburg Dock, May, 1900. By the end of the nineteenth century vast warehouses requiring new ding techniques were being built in the docks to store various products. The best known was the tobacco warehouse at the Stanley Dock h was probably the largest warehouse in the world when it was opened. It had a total floor space of about thirty-six acres and in its struction 27,000,000 bricks and about 6,000 tons of iron were used. Contemporaries were proud to point out that if St George's Hall was l bodily and dropped through the roof it would disappear from sight altogether.

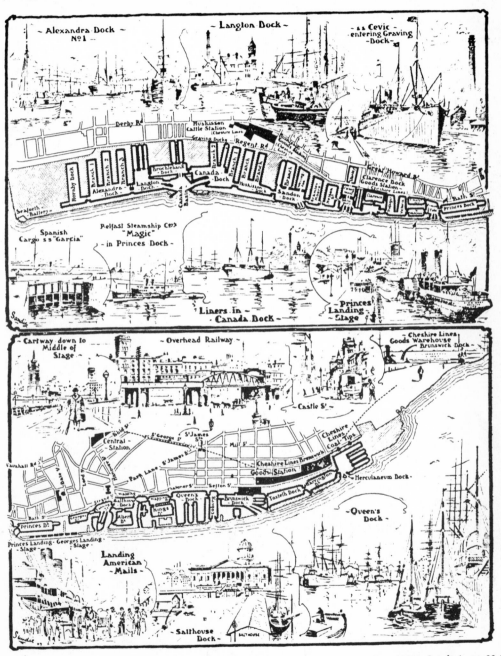

New routes and old acres—being the illustrated guide of the Cheshire Lines Committee (1902, London), pp 22-3.

The Bramley-Moore high level coal railway, c. 1900. The Bramley-Moore dock usually accommodated steamers trading to South America China. On its east and north sides there was this high level railway supported on arches. It was connected to the Lancashire and York. Railway and so brought coal from the Lancashire coalfields direct to the dock side.

...ton Graving Dock, July, 1899. This was one of many graving docks in the dock estate which was used for the maintenance and repair of ... Here were employed ships' painters, carpenters and fitters.

...ve: Workers standing on a caisson which was a dummy barge used in place of dock gates in an emergency. They were floated to the right ... and then sunk by filling with water.

...ve left: The men in the trench are widening the passage between the Langton and Alexandra Docks, July, 1899, to enable these docks to be ... by the new large vessels which were now plying the oceans. In this period considerable numbers of men were employed by the Dock ...ineer to modernise and extend the docks.

...w left: Men at work on one of the walls of the Coburg Dock. They are 'grouting', i.e., pointing the stones with tar to stop water seeping ...ugh.

Workmen being paid outside the dock yard, Coburg Dock, November 1902.

*system of casual employment used in the docks
the subject of much criticism from the late
teenth century. One such critic was Eleanor
bone, a member of the famous Rathbone family
h took a leading role in social reform in Liverpool
he nineteenth and twentieth centuries. The
wing extract is from Eleanor Rathbone's pamphlet
904 which examined employment for dockers. In
a clearing-house scheme involving registration of
ers and so controlling the supply of labour was
duced. This improved employment conditions
what but it was not until over half a century later
the system of casual employment for dockers was
ced.*

dock labour in Liverpool is casual, that is,
loyers have no, or very small, permanent staffs,
engage men day by day as they want them; the
imum period of employment being half a day.
usual way of hiring is to hold a "stand", either in
oad outside the dock wall, or inside by the sheds,
to the berth where the ship to be worked is lying.
men know the places where the different
loyers are wont to hold their stands, and group
selves there, shipmen in one place, quay porters
nother; and the foreman or wharfinger for each
ch, or in the case of small firms the employer
self, picks as many as he wants. Naturally he soon
to know the faces of the men who attend his stand
t frequently and whom he has found to work well,
takes them on in preference to strangers. It is his
rest to keep such men attached to his stand and to
ent them, even in slack times, from straying away
gether to other firms, so that they may be at hand
n a press comes. Hence he will "share out" the
x as far as possible amongst them. Thus, practices
sprung up which vary from firm to firm, but
h all tend to mitigate the purely casual nature of
employment. In small firms these practices are not
lly reduced to any formal system, but depend
rely on the eye and personal knowledge of the
, possessed by the foreman or employer. In the
e firms also this is sometimes the case, but more
n there is some more or less regular system of
nanent numbers. All firms give brass tallies or
s with numbers each week to the men they
loy, which serve to identify them when they claim
payment at the end of the week, but in the firms we
are speaking of the low numbers (that is those highest
on the list), are given to the best men, sometimes in
rude order of preference, and are retained from week
to week, while the mere casuals get shifting numbers.
All men holding permanent numbers are usually taken
on before resort is made to the casuals, but the
foreman in most firms seems to have full discretion to
put men to the jobs they are best suited for and to
share out the work amongst them as he pleases...

Whether constant numbers are given or not, nearly
every firm has a certain number of men who "follow"
its work, as long as it has any work for them. These the
foreman or wharfinger invariably alludes to as "our
men," and their ways of work and character are
probably as well known to him as if they were in
regular employ. Many of those specially attached to
one firm are said practically never to work for any one
else. Most dockers, however, move about a good deal
in search of work. If they know there will be no work
for them at the stand or stands where they are known,
they will ascertain by enquiry or from the newspaper
where a ship is expected, and will take their chance on
that stand of catching the foreman's eye. The exact
range of movement in search of work is very difficult
to ascertain and, of course, varies a great deal with the
energy and enterprise of the individual docker...

The foregoing outline of the general conditions of
labour at the Liverpool docks will, it is hoped, be
sufficient to make what follows intelligible to those
who have no personal acquaintance with the locality.
They will have gathered, what to all persons interested
in social conditions in Liverpool, as well as those
connected with the trade is a familiar fact, that the
greatest difficulty presented by dock labour—the
difficulty which makes it a "problem"— is the
excessive irregularity of the work. The amount of
loading and unloading to be done in the port at a
given time depends on a variety of causes, on weather
and tides, on the amount of cargo obtainable in
foreign ports, on the recurrent seasons for certain
imports and exports, on the general briskness of trade.

*Report of an inquiry into the conditions of dock
labour at the Liverpool docks*
(Liverpool, 1904), pp 8-9, 16.

Quiet rural scene at Aigburth, c. 1900.

Aigburth

Aigburth today is a populous suburb of Liverpool, situated about three miles south of the city centre. The name itself is derived from the Anglo Saxon and means 'the place of the oaks'. The photographs in this chapter were taken in Aigburth around the end of the nineteenth century by James Pinnington (1845-1922), a native of the area who was a master plumber by trade and also a keen amateur photographer who exhibited at several photographic exhibitions in Liverpool in the 1890s. When Pinnington took these photographs Aigburth still contained large

rural parts but this was changing and countryside was giving way to intensive housing to accomodate the expanding popula of Liverpool. Pinnington's work, theref provides us with a pleasant glimpse of a r Liverpool neighbourhood before its trans mation to a largely built-up suburb of the cit

This sort of change had, of course, been go on elsewhere in the countryside around Liverp throughout the nineteenth century. By beginning of Victoria's reign, the population the town had already spilt over from the

...molition work to part of the lower barn at Stanlawe Grange in progress, 1906.

...vnship around the port to Everton, Kirkdale ...d Toxteth. Rows of terrace housing now con-...ued to spread in these districts and from the ...ddle of the century this on-going urban ...pansion spread in the north side to places such ...Bootle, Walton, Seaforth and Waterloo, and in ...e east side to Anfield, Tuebrook and other ...ts of the West Derby township. Across the ...rsey urban expansion was taking place also in ...as such as Birkenhead and Wallasey. By the ...d of the century townships to the south, ...luding Allerton and Garston, the latter of ...ich embraced Aigburth, had become involved ...receiving Liverpool's spreading population.

...While the real growth in Aigburth's population ...ne from the end of the nineteenth century ...re had, nonetheless, been a steady trickle of ...ople from Liverpool to the area since the early ...t of the century. By the 1820s a number of ...erpool merchants had bought small estates in ...burth and throughout the century the area ...tinued to attract the attention of professional ...d business people who built there fine ...dences with spacious gardens. In Aigburth ...e terraces of cottages were built to house the ...ants from these residences.

Towards the end of the nineteenth century a number of the estates in Aigburth began to be broken up. Builders constructed terraces of four and six-roomed houses fitted with hot and cold water for skilled artisans from Liverpool, among whom Aigburth became a fashionable place to live, something which was now possible due to improved communications. The larger houses continued to fall to developers until by the 1930s there were few still in private occupation. In their place were neat roads of new housing, including many detached and semi-detached houses.

By the turn of the century Aigburth had already developed a number of social amenities for its growing population. There were several schools and churches and in 1901 the existing cocoa rooms and billiard hall, erected to provide an alternative to the public house for the working man, were replaced by the Peoples' Hall in Aigburth Vale, founded 'to provide for the inhabitants of the neighbourhood a club for mutual improvement, rational recreation and good fellowship', and offering a number of sports and activities such as billiards, football and socials. Aigburth became the home of Liverpool Cricket Club in 1881.

73

Front view of Stanlawe Grange, c. 1900. Parts of this farmhouse and its attached granary dated back to medieval times when the property neighbouring lands had been owned by the Cistercian monks of Stanlawe in the Wirral.

igburth Hall, home of J. A. Brodie, city engineer, c. 1900. This fine early Victorian mansion, with its spacious gardens and lawns, overlooking Aigburth cricket ground, was one of a number of large houses built in the area in the course of the nineteenth century for prosperous erpool merchants and professional people. By the end of the century, however, a number of these estates had already been broken up to ke way for new housing development. This fate did not befall Aigburth Hall until the mid 1930s when it was purchased and demolished by velopers.

Aigburth Road, with workmen laying cobble stones alongside newly constructed electric tramlines, c. 1902. By the 1830s there were reg
omnibus services from the town centre to Aigburth and in the 1870s a horse tramline was extended from Dingle to Aigburth Vale, althoug
dispute between the tramline company and Toxteth local board interrupted its effective running for a long time. The electric tramway sysi
was extended to Aigburth in 1899. The development of transport facilities in the course of the nineteenth and early twentieth centuries was t
to the growth of these areas around Liverpool.

extent of the tramlines around Liverpool and
cially to and from Aigburth by the early twentieth
ury can be gauged by this short extract on the
ways from a guide book of 1912:

tric Tramways spread their tentacles, octopus-like,
n the centre of the city to all its boundaries. The
icipal termini are the Pier Head, St George's
scent, and the Old Haymarket. In all there are
nty-four routes, and every part of the city can be
kly and easily reached at small cost. The
poration acquired the old horse tramway system in
8 for £600,000. There are now 116 miles of track,
rated by five hundred cars, carrying two and a
rter million passengers per week an average
ance of 2½ miles for a penny. Many of the cars are
ed with upper-deck covers, adding greatly both to
r convenience and earning power, without to any
ous degree interfering with the amenities of outside
elling in fine weather.

An innovation was the introduction on certain
routes of first-class cars, the fares being slightly higher
than those by the ordinary cars. The first-class trams
were luxuriously equipped, and their patronage was of
such a nature that they have been put on other routes.

Aintree, Fazakerley and Aigburth. Through fare,
4*d.* Cars every 4 or 5 minutes. Aintree terminus
adjoins the racecourse. The cars pass along Warbreck
Moor, Walton Vale—where, at the *Black Bull,* the
Fazakerley line joins—Rice Lane and County Road.
Spellow Lane leads to Stanley Park. Thence *via*
Walton Road, Kirkdale Road, Scotland Road and
Byrom Street to the Old Haymarket, in the centre of
the city. From the Haymarket *via* Whitechapel,
Paradise Street, Park Lane, St James's Street and
Place and Park Road to Dingle. Thence by Aigburth
Road to Aigburth terminus, near Sefton Park.

A pictorial and descriptive guide to Liverpool,
Birkenhead, New Brighton, the Wirral etc.
[London, 1912, eleventh edition], pp 32-3.

w: 1909 advertisement for another type of transport.

MOTORS

THE
LARGEST
AND MOST
CONVENIENT

GARAGE

IS

L. PERCY PICKERING'S

BENNS GARDENS,
REDCROSS STREET,

Liverpool.

Cars.

DAIMLER.   DARRACQ.
SIDDELEY.   CALTHORPE.

Scene at Aigburth hotel, May 1898, on the occasion of trials for heavy traffic motor vehicles for use in the docks, organised by the Liverp branch of the Self Propelled Traffic Association. The two motor cars in the photograph are probably judges' cars.

...ree cyclists in front of Aigburth hotel, 1902. The two cyclists on the left have racing bikes with drop handles while the cyclist on the right has ...ordinary roadster; all three are dressed in appropriate cycling gear. Perhaps they are members of a cycling club on a day outing from Liverpool ...the rural peace of Aigburth.

A typical court off Burlington Street.

Houses, roads and drains

In the late eighteenth century observers regarded Liverpool as one of the healthiest towns in the kingdom, renowned for the salutary effects of her brisk breezes and pure air. By the mid nineteenth century, however, the borough was not regarded so favourably, for the tremendous growth of Liverpool's population due to her increased trade and the arrival of thousands of people fleeing the great Irish famine had led to severe overcrowdir and unhygienic housing conditions as well many other problems such as the inadequacy the existing water supply and sewerage facilitie In response to this situation nineteenth centu Liverpool introduced many innovations in th field of public health and borough administratio some of which were forerunners of simil velopments in the rest of Britain, such as the establishment of public baths and wash-houses in the 1840s and the formation of the district nurse service in 1859. In this whole area of public health administration an important step was the 1846 Liverpool Sanitary Act which established several new borough posts including that of medical officer of health and of borough engineer.

It is with the duties of this latter official and his successor, the city engineer, that we are concerned in this chapter. The photographs, by an unknown member of the city engineer's department in the period 1890-1912, cast an interesting light on the activities of the department and the problems and day-to-day matters with which it was concerned. These photographs, taken for the use of the department's officials, show a side of Liverpool life not recorded by other photographers but which touches on many aspects of importance to the lives of Liverpool's people.

By the 1890s the activities of the city engineer and his department had expanded considerably from the 1840s, a development reflecting the growing involvement of the corporation in affairs relating to public health and town development. The water supply and refuse collection for the borough were taken from the care of various private and local bodies and placed under municipal control; in both these areas the engineer's department played an important part in organising matters effectively, although the water supply was eventually placed under a new department in the corporation. Sewerage and the widening and paving of roads were other responsibilities of the engineer.

A further area of importance in which the city engineer's department became more and more involved was the clearing of slums and construction of corporation housing, tasks in which it was assisted by the city surveyor's department. By the beginning of the twentieth century official thinking on these problems had developed considerably from the time of the founding of the borough engineer's post. From the 1840s a number of important new housing by-laws were introduced controlling the construction of new houses and efforts were made to close some of the worst cellar and slum dwellings, although slum clearance and the building of corporation houses were much slower in coming.

In 1864 the corporation acquired powers to demolish insanitary houses but little action was taken until the 1880s when rising public concern over slum conditions, aroused by the findings of a parliamentary housing commission and a series of articles in the *Liverpool Daily Post* in 1882 entitled 'Squalid Liverpool', led to a more vigorous clearance policy being carried out. By the turn of the century about 12,000 insanitary dwellings had been cleared and by 1914 a further 9000 approximately had been pulled down or closed.

The corporation was reluctant to take on a municipal housing construction policy and in 1869 built the St Martin's Cottages as an example to private builders of the sort of artisans' dwellings they wished to see erected in the borough. This effort, however, failed to bring results and in 1885 the Victoria Square workingmen's dwellings were constructed followed by the Juvenal buildings in 1890. From 1900 a much more active new housing policy was followed which led to the construction of 2392 dwellings between 1900 and 1914. This left severe housing problems still to be tackled in Liverpool but it should be noted that in absolute numbers of municipal houses built, Liverpool was ahead of nearly every other municipality in Britain.

During the period which these photographs cover, the city engineer was John Alexander Brodie. Born in 1858, he was appointed to this post in 1898 and held it until 1926. An associate professor of engineering in Liverpool University, his most significant contribution to the city was the development of Liverpool's first ring road Queen's Drive, on which construction began in 1903. Brodie died in 1934.

Above: This photograph, taken in 1908, shows the redevelopment taking place at Pier Head on the site of the old George's dock. On the le, the rising form of the Mersey Docks and Harbour Board offices, the first of three imposing and magnificent buildings to grace this site. In fr of these new offices are the foundations of the Royal Liver Building, designed by W. Aubrey Thomas and opened in 1911, which was one of first examples in the world of a multi-storeyed reinforced concrete construction. The third building in this area was the headquarters of Cunard shipping company, built during the First World War, also of reinforced concrete. Statutory town planning was introduced formall; Liverpool only in 1909 with the passing of the Housing and Town Planning Act of that year, but due to its various building and traffic by-l; the corporation, through the city engineer's department, had taken a considerable interest for some time in developments such as those at I Head.

Above right: Laying the tramlines in Park Road, July 1898. The corporation took over the city's tramway system in 1897 and steps were s; taken for the electrification of the system, a matter which involved the widening of many roads to provide for the laying of double tracks. first route chosen for electrification was from Dingle to South Castle Street, via Park Road. The track was laid under the supervision of the engineer, J. A. Brodie, and he personally instructed the drivers on the occasion on 14 November 1898 when the first electric trams came into service on the line. Many thousands of people turned out to watch the first trams in action.

Below right: Corporation water wagon at Commutation Row, April 1905. The whole of the public street works in the city was carried out by city engineer's department and included the laying, widening and cleaning of streets. The purpose of the wagon in the photograph was to w the streets and so lay the dust, thus allowing it to be easily swept away. Other corporation wagons were used for collecting refuse from st; orderly boys, who swept the central part of the city. In some of the poorer districts, the streets and passages were washed regularly to remove and unhygienic matter from the street surface.

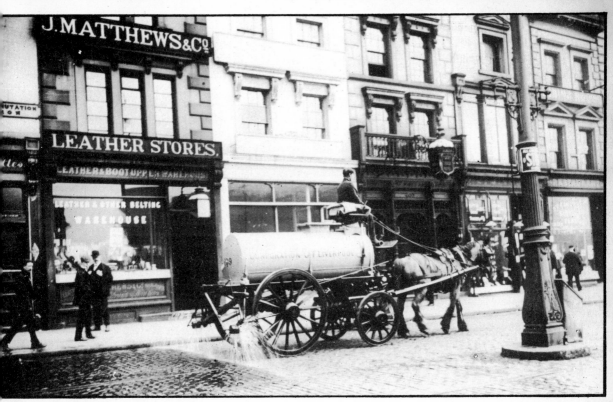

Above: A court in Saltney Street, 1906:

Courts, such as the one featured here, were a major feature of working class housing in nineteenth century Liverpool. A typical court consiste[...]
a narrow strip of land, usually only thirty feet wide, on which there were two rows of three-storey dwellings, each with a depth and fronta[...]
about ten feet; both ends of the court were often blocked by other buildings and access was only by a narrow passageway. Frequently six[...]
seventy persons would be found in a single court, all using the one water tap and two conveniences at each end of the court, in full view [...]
the other residents. In the mid 1860s it was reckoned that there were over three thousand courts, housing around one fifth of Liverp[...]
population but, due to corporation action, by 1895 the number had been halved and by 1914 there were under four hundred. This typ[...]
accomodation was to be found mainly in the Vauxhall and Scotland Road areas. A graphic description of life in these courts and other par[...]
Liverpool slums at the turn of the century can be found in Pat O'Mara's The autobiography of an Irish slummy *(London, 1934; reprint [...]*
1967).

seup of ashbin in a Saltney Street court, 1909 — with a few young observers! These bins were specially designed by the city engineer in 1898 were widely distributed to courts and private houses in an attempt to improve waste disposal and sanitary conditions.

Lionel Street, 1905. The dwellings in this street appear superior to those in the Saltney Street court. The street is neatly cobbled and has o
access. But it is likely that the dwellings would have been overcrowded. These houses have cellars, as did many houses in working class ar
which were occupied by the poorest inhabitants of the city. Efforts were made to close these cellars, but in spite of some success by
authorities, many were still occupied at the turn of the century due to lack of alternative accommodation for the really poor. Notice the chick
wandering freely around the street.

*e wretched conditions in dwellings such as these in
* 1880s was the subject of a series of articles based
* an enquiry by the* Liverpool Daily Post *in October
*82, entitled 'Squalid Liverpool', which resulted in
*w steps being taken to improve housing conditions.
e following is an extract from the paper:

e docks, with Liverpool's great fleet within their
tes, are close at hand. Over the stones which pave
e street lorries and waggons incessantly rumble,
aring their freight of merchandise from the ships
ich have brought it from distant shores, or to the
ssels which will scatter it all over the earth. The
eet is always thronged with busy men, who hurry to
d fro—some clerks, some warehousemen, some
isans, and a very large number of simple dock
ourers...

To find out what squalor is one should walk north-
rds along Great Howard-street until the Stanley
ck is reached. On the right-hand side of the way
ere is a street called Sherwood-street. This will do
ry well for a beginning. It is palatial and salubrious
comparison with some of the streets we shall after-
rds visit; still it will afford the inquirer plenty of
od for consideration...

Let us walk up Sherwood-street. The women as
ual manifest a good deal of interest in the doings of
e strangers. They are of all ages and all sorts, but all
e very tattered and nearly all very dirty. At the top of
e street is a sewer grid merrily puffing off clouds of
am, which the wind blows through the dilapidated
ndows of the houses close by. On one side of the
eet there are a couple of rickety high wooden gates
inted a cheerful black. It is not necessary to peep
rough to discover what is inside. The rustic odour
ich is wafted across the street proclaims the exist-
ce of a shippon or a stable. On the opposite side is a
rresponding pair of doors opening into a yard which
bounded by the high railway embankment....

Passing downwards, one comes to No. 24. This
use is worth a visit. It is inhabited by a chimney-
eep and his family. The house, it should be noticed,
opened through at the back, and there appears to be
* reason, if proper precautions were observed, why
ver should find victims here. The parlour is entered
om the street up three or four steps. It contains a
oden bench, a bed, and one chair. The family con-
ts of four adults and five children, all of the most

hopelessly-squalid type. When we visited the place the
sweep occupied the single chair which his household
effects included. On his knee he nursed a little child,
and his wife, standing by him, carried another in her
arms. The pair were young and pleasant spoken, but
all wore that wearied, indifferent expression on their
faces which is indicative of extreme poverty. There is
no water in the house, and as a matter of course no
gas, which is a luxury unknown in squalid Liverpool.
Above this parlour there are two bedrooms; below it is
a cellar, which is sub-let, and contains a bed.

Disease must frequently be traced to the occupation
of these cellars, but it is a fact that cannot be over-
looked that when they are closed they frequently
become more dangerous and offensive than before.
Not infrequently they degenerate into a sort of extem-
porised ashpit, where the accumulation of rubbish and
dirt goes on for years, till some tenant enters, and,
finding that the cellar will hold no more, lodges a
complaint, has it cleared out, and then steadily
commences to fill it up again. A letter has been
handed to us written by a well-known philanthropic
lady, bearing a name historical in Liverpool. The
writer states that there are 10,000 inhabited cellars still
remaining in this city. In these she believes thirty or
forty thousand children must be growing up to a
maturity of wretchedness and vice. It is very difficult
to ascertain definitely whether cellars are so generally
occupied as this lady supposes. The inhabitants of
houses everywhere will assert positively and emphat-
ically that only one family resides in the house, and
"is only used for washing." Parenthetically it may be
noted that these people, dirty as they are and still
dirtier as their clothes are, seem to be incessantly
engaged in washing. What they wash is best known to
themselves. Certainly it is neither their faces nor their
clothes. To discover whether a house is sub-let or not
requires a good deal of sharp cross-examination. It
may then be ultimately elicited, as in the case of this
sweep's house, that the cellar is separately occupied.

Above: Workingmen's dwellings at Whittle Street, 1912. Facing page: Holly Road, 1913. In response to the appalling housing conditions corporation introduced various local acts effecting new house construction and existing housing accommodation from the 1840s onwards. A of 1864 allowed the corporation to demolish insanitary dwellings but only piecemeal work was carried out in this area until the 1880s p because there was little other accommodation for the people displaced from these dwellings. Municipal artisan dwellings were first erecte

69 but only limited housing was provided by the corporation until the end of the century when a more vigorous policy was pursued. These ...ellings in Whittle Street were constructed probably in the 1890s while those in Holly Road have obviously just been constructed and the older ...ildings they replaced have still to be demolished totally.

ove: Smithdown Road, c. 1900. Off this main road there existed many other examples of the type of housing seen in Dicken's Street.

ove left: Dicken's Street, 1911. This street is typical of the very many new streets constructed by private developers in Liverpool in the last arter of the nineteenth and early twentieth century. Under municipal regulations they were laid out in planned parallel lines and houses had have various features such as backyards and a certain amount of light.

ow left: Queen's Drive, from Menlove Avenue, 1911. The city engineer was the originator of the Queen's Drive scheme which was the city's t ring road. Begun in 1903, six miles of Queen's Drive had been constructed by 1912, with numerous radial roads. This was an extremely portant step by the corporation and helped alleviate traffic congestion which was increasing, largely due to the introduction of the motor car, hough when this photograph was taken, traffic was obviously not very busy in this part of the city!

Entitled 'The fairyland of dreams, Mann Island', this wonderful photograph was taken by Richard Eastham, c. 1904.

Various views

In this final chapter we have included work by a number of photographers on a variety of subjects. Unfortunately, information on the lives of most of these artists is scanty. The first is Richard Eastham, who was responsible for an album of photographs of Liverpool street scenes and characters, taken around the turn of the century. Another photographer who also interested himself in this subject in the same period was G.

Lascelles. A photograph from the studio Brown, Barnes and Bell has been included; t firm had rooms in Bold Street and was one of t leading commercial photographic studios Liverpool in the late nineteenth and ea twentieth centuries.

Justin McCarthy, who died in 1940, worked the Liverpool Education Office and was respo sible for six albums of photographs on Liverpo

e smallest house in England — 95 High Street, Wavertree, 1902 (Eastham).

id its surrounding area, shot between about)10 and 1930. His three photographs in this hapter are rather unusual and show the city early the morning and later in the evening.

Finally we have selected four photographs from book written by James Granville Legge and ublished in 1914, entitled *The thinking hand or ractical education in the elementary school* .ondon). Legge, who was director of education i Liverpool between 1906 and 1921, urged that greater attention should be given in schools to teaching children practical skills. He included a number of photographs showing children and work in Liverpool schools and we have used some of these. The book does not say who took the photographs and they may not have been Legge's own work but in any case they give us an interesting view of activity in some of the schools at this time.

Almshouses, Cambridge Street, 1901 (Eastham). These almshouses were built originally for poor sailors or their widows. They were closed d in 1911.

...ildren outside the rooms of the Food and Betterment Association, Lime Kiln Lane, c. 1904. This association was one of the numerous ...ritable bodies in Liverpool at this time. Its chief object was to supply halfpenny and free meals to school children and others in the poorest ...tricts of Liverpool, Bootle and Birkenhead. It also sought to supply the young and adult sick poor of these areas with special food and to ...vide 'slum and alley concerts' during the summer.

above: Bookstalls in the old Haymarket, at the foot of St John's gardens, c. 1900 (Lascelles).

above left: St John's church and gardens, St George's hall, the museum and the Picton reading room, c. 1890 (Brown, Barnes and Bell).

below left: The last of St John's church, 1898 (Lascelles). Following the demolition of the church various statues of Liverpool notables were erected in the garden, including those of William Rathbone, Father Nugent, Canon Major Lester and Gladstone.

Learning practical skills at school: top, making and repairing shoes at Penrhyn Street school; below, learning to sew at Oakes Street sc
right, 'housewifery' lessons at Harrington School (Legge).

98

Liverpool had few of the educational endowments and long established institutions of other cities like Birmingham and Sheffield. However, a number of important educational developments took place in Liverpool. The first school in England for the education and training of the blind was established in Liverpool in 1791 and the school for the deaf and dumb in Oxford Street was one of the earliest institutions of its kind in the country. When the Elementary Education Act, 1870, came into operation, Liverpool was one of the few large towns where the schools already provided by voluntary agencies, and especially by the main religious denominations, met the estimated requirements.

After 1870 the work of the voluntary bodies was supplemented by that of the Liverpool school board. By 1903 there were 156 schools in the city comprising forty-three board and 113 voluntary schools. Liverpool also took a leading role in the introduction to the elementary schools of practical instruction in woodwork, metal work and other crafts for boys, cookery, laundry and housework for girls. The book by Legge from which these photographs are taken sought to promote the importance of manual crafts both for personal development and the skills it provided.

'Emphatically, a most efficient place, this Liverpool, glossy and high stepping, at once elegant and active. And with nightfall it emerges as a place of quite exceptional loveliness. That checked curve of the receding buildings, giving the prospect depth, without diminution, grades the lights without disparting them, knits them together, both the near and the far, into one exquisitely modulated chorus.'

J. H. Hay and Dixon Scott, *Liverpool* (London, 1907), pp 51-2.

Ruins of Everton toffee shop on Everton Brow, c. 1884. This was the shop established by Molly Bushell in 1753 where the famous Everton t... was first made and from which Everton Football Club takes the nickname of the 'Toffees'. (Photographer unknown.)

Bibliography

Many books and articles were consulted in the preparation of this book but the following were especially important.

George Chandler. *Victorian and Edwardian Liverpool and the North West from old photographs.* London, 1972.

Howard Channon. *Portrait of Liverpool.* London, 1970.

City of Liverpool official handbook. Liverpool, 1909.

Quentin Hughes. *Seaport.* London, 1964.

F. E. Hyde. *Liverpool and the Mersey.* Newton Abbot, 1971.

Bill Jay. *Victorian cameraman: Francis Frith's views of rural England, 1850-98.* Newton Abbot, 1973.

D. Caradog Jones (ed.). *The social survey of Mers... side.* Vol. 1. Liverpool, 1934.

A pictorial and descriptive guide to Liverpool, Birk... head, New Brighton, the Wirral, etc. Ward Lock Co. London, various editions.

Public health congress, Liverpool, 1903. Liverpo... 1903.

Sea Breezes.

The story of Aigburth, Liverpool. Liverpool, 1953.

E. L. Taplin. 'Dock labour at Liverpool...' in *Tra... actions of the Historic Society of Lancashire a... Cheshire.* Vol. 27, 1978, pp 133-54.

B. D. White. *A history of the corporation of Liverpo... 1835-1914.* Liverpool, 1951.

...d Philharmonic Concert Hall, Hope Street, c. 1910. (Photographer unknown.)

Acknowledgements

...would like to thank the many people who have ...d us with this book. Our work was greatly ...ed by the information and help so willingly given ...iss Janet Smith and the staff of the Liverpool ...al Library local history and record office. Mr ... Taylor of the photographic service of the joint ...ies of social and environmental studies and arts ...verpool University provided us with first class ...s of the required photographs. Mr Ron Boughton ...e Mersey Dock and Harbour Board kindly assisted ...relation to the docks' photographs. Miss Bernie ...irth gave invaluable assistance in the research for ...ook. Mr Michael McCaughan and Mr Tony Ryan ...d identifiy our ship photographs. Finally we ...d like to thank our parents for their assistance and ...iragement.

...e photographs in the chapter on the docks came from the archives of the Mersey Docks and Harbour Board who have kindly allowed us to use them here. All the other photographs were selected from the very large photographic collection in the record office and local history department of Liverpool Central Library. For permission to use the photographs on the work of the city engineer's department we are grateful to the city engineer. For permission to reproduce the other photographs we wish to thank the city librarian.

For kind permission to reprint copyright material, acknowledgements are made to the following: The Gallery Press for the extract from *Her Benny*; the editor of *Sea Breezes* for the extract from this magazine; the Society of Authors for the extract from John Masefield; A. & C. Black Ltd for the extract from J. H. Hay and Dixon Scott's *Liverpool*.

May Day parade, May 1914 — a festive scene in Lime Street not long before the outbreak of the First World War and the end of a peaceful prosperous era in Liverpool's history. (Photographer unknown.)